Every Day in the USA: 30 Black Moments

EVERY DAY IN THE USA:
30 Black Moments

BY ANIKA NAILAH
ILLUSTRATIONS BY C. ANDREW WILLIAMS

New York, NY

First Printing August 2018

Book Design and Cover Art: C. Andrew Williams

Illustrations: C. Andrew Williams

To all the Black folks in the USA who rise above their sadness and pain and still find joy.

Acknowledgements

I want to thank my ancestors and parents for all the sacrifices they made for me. Many thanks as well to all our pre-readers who muddled through our early draft and took the time to offer invaluable feedback and insights. Real love to C. Andrew Williams, my fellow artist and newfound friend, who worked his tail off to make this project a reality. Much props as well to Alexa Palacios, my publicist, who believed in this book from the beginning and without whom, it may never have been fully birthed into the world. A very special thanks to Malcolm Thomas, who, with his keen sense of chemistry and taste gave me the gift of a top shelf creative team, and to my partner, who was there at the conception of this idea and encouraged me to get it out of my head and get busy.

--Anika Nailah

I'd like to thank my entire family and all of my friends for the rock solid support they've given me as I continue my journey through life as an illustrator. Thanks to Anika Nailah, the author of this book, who invited me to join her on this project, and has taught me so much about the creative process in general. The completion of this book has influenced my work for the better by encouraging me to put even more of myself into everything I do.

--C. Andrew Williams

Also by Anika Nailah:

Free & Other Stories
National Liberation Poetry Tour Experience
Gumbo: A Celebration of African American Writing (contributor)

Table of Contents

Introduction (or How Langston Hughes Found Me)

At 60 years of age, you give up on some questions and start asking others. As a Pocasset Wampanoag African American woman raised in African American culture, however, I remain invested in what I hope words can still do. As I wrote this book, I wondered which words were needed in this Age of Trump where racism has been publicly re-enfranchised from The Ultimate White House to houses of everyday white folks. I contemplated if words would be enough to keep me or any other black bodies afloat while the cold and mighty undertow of white supremacy converged to pull us under once more. If words alone were not sufficient, what else was needed?

It's the morning of July 7, 2016. I'm in a room with about 30 teens from all over the United States, almost all brown, black, or indigenous. We're on the campus of Hampshire College in Amherst, Massachusetts. Last night, near St. Paul, Minnesota, Philando Castile, an African American school cafeteria supervisor, seat belt on, was shot dead in his car in front of his 4-year-old daughter and his girlfriend. The police officer who shot him said he feared for his life. The night before that, Alton Sterling, also African American, was killed by police outside a supermarket in Baton Rouge, Louisiana.

I am in this room with other adults to hold space so the young people can make sense of what has happened. It is a moment in a longstanding social justice organization called The Encampment. The youth are full of rage, grief, and the feeling that floods your belly when you're fighting despair.

One teen recalls the team of counselors that arrived at the Sandy Hook Elementary School in Newtown, Connecticut after the December 14, 2012 shooting, and cries out, "Where's our therapy? How come no one comes to our schools?" They talk of how unsafe they feel walking down the streets of their neighborhoods as they're stalked by police, followed by clerks in places where they spend money or intend to, and how closely they are monitored and largely feared in the school buildings they attend every day. They speak of Trayvon, Tamir, Rekia, Sandra, Aiyana, Sean. I can barely keep up with all the names. Young people and children who look like them. Same scenario over and over again, typically ending with a dead black body and full acquittal. Voices break. Tears wet cheeks.

I thought I was prepared. Overcome by the cumulative pain of so many and the many they represented in that one safe space, I found myself sobbing.

But the tears were seeds. *If words alone were not suffi-*

cient, what else was needed? The book was growing inside me then, even though I didn't know it.

Many months later, I found myself asking: *what if ordinary, familiar moments of our existence could be expressed in illustrations and minimal text?* Moments that could illustrate in simple terms, the complicated truths of African American lives. Our truths. Us telling our own stories. Could this be a "room" in our country we might all be able to enter? It was then that I remembered a book a dear white friend had given me many years ago by Langston Hughes, *Black Misery*.

Spring of 1967. Langston Hughes begins work on his final book project. According to Robert G. O'Meally, Hughes had been approached by Paul S. Erickson, who had previously published a highly popular series of picture-and-caption books by white suburbanite author, Suzanne Heller—*Misery* (1964), *More Misery* (1965), and *Misery Loves Company* (1967). Using drawings and sentences to portray many miserable moments of embarrassment from childhood and adolescence, the Heller books were for and about children. Erickson wrote to Hughes: "…there might well be great value and marketability in a similar book in the series which would be based entirely upon Negro 'miseries'."

So, Hughes gets to work writing several one sentence vignettes through the eyes of a black boy, depicting everyday life in the United States of America in the 1960s. His down-to-earth yet profound descriptions later became *Black Misery*. And, as in the first Heller book, each one-sentence page of *Black Misery* began with: "Misery is…" On May 22, 1967, Brother Langston dies of complications from prostate cancer in New York City's Hell's Kitchen at Polyclinic Hospital, having completed 27 of the 45 planned scenarios.

Published a few years later, with Hughes' 27 sentences standing as the text of the book, *Black Misery* is marketed as planned as children's literature. Surely schooling more than children about the impact of racism, the book's stark, black and white illustrations by Arouni that accompany Hughes' words create an artful collection that reflects the humor, sadness, and irony of the often surreal existence of African Americans in the 1960s.

Perfect, I thought. Why not pick up the thread? 50 years later, in 21st Century USA, what are the everyday encounters of African Americans? I asked myself. How different are our moments from the ones reflected in the time of Hughes' book?

Born in the 20th century, I recalled how my own life had been filled with moments where I carried the burden of proof of my worthiness— the white girl who called me a racial slur on the school bus in the white, suburban neighborhood where we lived, and her mother who defended her, the white boys who refused to hold my hand when we square danced in gym class, the effigy of a black body burned near our Long Island home. I remembered my adult years in this century when I sat in front of the TV screen or computer screen, took deep breaths, cursed and cried. When 17-year-old Trayvon was shot to death in a gated community in Sanford, Florida. When Troy Davis was executed by lethal injection in Savannah, Georgia. When 19-year-old Michael Brown lay dead and uncovered on Canfield Drive in Ferguson, Missouri for 4 hours. When 17-year-old Lennon Lacy was found hanging by two belts from a swing set in a field in Bladenboro, North Carolina. When three Black trans women--one, Tiara Richmond, 24 in Chicago, and both Chyna Doll Dupree, 31, and Ciara McElveen, 25 in New Orleans, were all murdered within days of each other.

I could not deny the relentless hatred of black people in the United States. This continues to be further demonstrated by the quality of so many of our lives, which are constrained by lack of access to basic human resources like decent housing, education, and healthcare (to name a few). Looking unflinchingly at this reality spoke to an even deeper mass murder beyond the outright killing of our bodies—the impact of these generation-to-generation assaults on our humanity and our collective psyche. I was forced to acknowledge that the tenacious nature of racial oppression remained the undercurrent in 2017, just as it had been in the 1960s (and ever since our kidnapping), notwithstanding superficial, contemporary appearances, even in moments of joy, wonder, and humor.

For this reason, as in *Black Misery*, I included a youthful perspective, but unlike Hughes' book, chose to broaden the book's lens beyond the eyes of a child. I thought it might be possible to show what it looks like to live with racism, cradle-to-grave, while white folks skip by in oblivion. I wanted the book to show glimpses of our navigation of this inequity of awareness and circumstance in the full spectrum of our lives. Most importantly, I wanted it to show how we maintain our humanity and sense of humor through it all.

What interested me most were the monologues we have in our minds and the dialogues we have on street corners, in living rooms, in workplaces, and in virtual spaces all over the USA. The silent monologue when yet again, a white colleague confuses us with someone whose only resemblance to us is the color of their skin. Or the one when our name is mispronounced more often than it is said correctly. The words that pop up like cartoon bubbles when we walk or drive through a white neighborhood, hoping we make it back home to our spaces of color (or back to our oasis in the desert of whiteness we are forced to live in if we've "made it"). In all cases, these exchanges are familiar to us. We wrestle with them. Every. Single. Day.

So, why tell you something you already know? Well, sometimes, bringing what is familiar out into the light surfaces insights we didn't know we had. I believe that seeing and hearing these images and words in a new light might help us more clearly recognize the pathology and absurdity of racism, and the situations we don't create, yet find ourselves in. Amidst the insanity of everyday racism, perhaps we can realize that *we are not insane*. The circumstances may be, but we are not.

Clearly, the circumstances surrounding the latter days of this book's conception were insane. Like the rest of us, I struggled to live through the bizarre, yet historic phenomenon of Donald Trump taking his place as the 45th President of the United States. [I still do.] Thankfully, in that time of unimaginable daily events, the process of creation had a way of challenging reality's hold on my sense of what is possible. Collaborating with C. Andrew Williams, my gifted illustrator, to whom I am forever indebted, was the best dose of counter-reality I could have hoped for. He understood the concept of the book right away. Though he was of African American descent, male, and from the 1980s Deep South, and I, female from 1950s New England, many of our experiences were similar. We laughed, empathized, and consoled each other, as he jumped right in and illustrated the first and secondhand vignettes of both our lives.

Consequently, if you identify as a person of color, I hope these pages remind you that you are not alone. Let this book be the community where you can feel safe to be unapologetically who you are, even if what follows might make you angry, want to shake your head, or even laugh out loud. If you're white, the book might make you wince or leave you bewildered. But then, what, white reader? Will you allow your experience to move you enough to live a more socially just life? Will you sustain your curiosity to seek deeper humility and understanding, and ultimately take action *every day* to dismantle white supremacy inside and outside of you?

Ultimately, my hope, no matter who you are, is that the illustrations and words will touch something in you that makes you want to share them with someone you care about. The fact that the vignettes depict situations not often freely shared across race in this, our 21st century of living together in the United States of America, is a sad commentary on how far we have not come. Finally, I also wanted to pay tribute, not only to the great Langston Hughes for the vibrant, humorous, rich legacy he gave us, but also to all of us who so graciously endure the microaggressions of racism each day and thrive and thrive and thrive despite them.

On the very day that I write these words, Police Officer Yanez has been exonerated in the murder of Philando Castile.

May the themes of this book contribute to us having the conversations we *must* have within and across race, then lead us beyond talk to the actions against oppression that this time in our history compels us to take.

--Anika Nailah
June 16, 2017

THE TENDER YEARS

White Passenger:
Isn't he darling!

Black Mother *(thinking)*:
Mmm-hmmm. He get a little bigger, you be clutching your purse tighter than that.

TAXI
THANK YOU

Black Mother *(thinking)*:
Where do I begin?

WELCOME BACK!

ADOLESCENCE

Black Father:
Boy, you know you can't wear no hoodie. Take the umbrella.

Black Teen:
I'm *good*, dad! Don't need that!

White Police Officer:
Come on over and have some fun!

Black Boy:
Uh...I think I hear my mama calling.

AIR
MEET YOUR LOCAL POLICE!
SAFETY
County Fair
BOOTH # 11
A.C.P.D.

Black Teen:
Maybe today I can just be invisible.

THE COLLEGE YEARS

White Professor:
Glad you're taking this course! By the way, we do have a Campus Tutorial Center.

Black Student:
So why didn't you make that announcement to the whole class...?

Black Girlfriend #1:
We gonna be late!

Black Girlfriend #2:
Hold up! Need to put my earrings on. Don't want the cops mistaking me for a Black man.

Black Girlfriend #1 *(sarcastically)***:**
Yeah, *that'll* work. When's the last time you watched the news?

Black Friend #1:
Don't worry, you'll ace this interview. You're ready!

Black Friend #2:
But...do I look too Black?

HUMAN
RESOURCES

MAKING A LIVING

White Presenter to Audience:
Having a photograph on your website increases the likelihood people will do business with you.

Black Businessman:
Hmmm...

YOUR
BUSINESS WEBSITE
AND YOU!

White Woman to Bi-Racial Woman:
So...what are you?

Bi-Racial Woman *(thinking)***:**
A human being.

Reporter on Television:
The suspect, alleged to be responsible for four assaults and an armed robbery, was apprehended yesterday evening.

Black Employee *(thinking)***:**
Thank God he wasn't Black.

NOTICE BOARD
APPREHENDED
ARMED ROBBERY
ASSAULT

White Woman:
Did I pronounce it correctly?

Black Woman *(thinking)*:
I know she didn't just call me "Shaniqua."

ANIKA

Black Employee #1:
So he says to me, "I've decided to be your ally. Here's what I want you to do..."

Black Employee #2:
Incredible.

White Woman:
She's so articulate.

Black Woman #1:
That went well. Especially when she said...

Both:
"I'm not racist!"

Black Employee #1:
Let's leave early, before they get too drunk.

Black Employee #2:
I was thinking the same thing.

CONGRATULATIONS
TEAM!!!

MOVIN' ON UP

Black Family:
Seriously?!

Westfield, MA
WHIP CITY

White Realtor:
This is a really good neighborhood!

Black Couple *(thinking)*:
And what's the cost...?

Black Parent #1 *(referring to the white teacher)***:**
She doesn't have a clue.

Black Parent #2:
Yeah...it's gonna be a long year.

ABCDEFGHIJKLMNOPQRSTUVWXYZ

Black Man *(thinking)*:
Hope I don't get arrested.

Black Neighbor:
Good to see you this morning! Tell your partner I said hello.

White Neighbor:
I'll give him your regards! *(Turning to his black dog)* C'mon, Sambo. Let's go inside.

Black Woman:
My car's...not...ready?

White Mechanic:
Calm down, lady. If you insist, you can drive it with the broken tail light, and bring it back tomorrow or...

Black Woman:
No, *you* can drive it with that broken tail light. Remember Sandra Bland?

White Mechanic:
Uh...Sandra who?

CHILLIN'

Black Diner #1:
Is it my imagination? Or...

Black Diner #2:
Nope. You ain't crazy.

Black Man *(thinking)*:
Should I jog...? Or walk...?

STOP

White Hipster:
Hey man, I get the whole Indian aesthetic thing. It's pretty cool. I'm like, one-eighth Indian.

Black Native American:
You gotta be kidding me...!

Black Muslim Woman *(slowly)*:
I want...

White Barista:
Yes?! Yes?!

Black Muslim Woman:
...a mocha latte. And BREATHE.

Black Partner:
Would you mind standing here for a second and pretending you're hailing a cab?

White Partner:
Uh...sure. Why...?

TAXI
TAXI
TAXI

THE GOLDEN YEARS

Trump on TV:
I've never had a problem with the Blacks!

Older Black Woman:
Lord, have mercy. It's the perfect Oreo cookie!

electronics

Old Black Man:
I can't believe I'm still dealing with this damn mess.

Peaceful Brook Home

AMEN

Black Person #1:
It's so nice to not have to explain myself.

All at the table:
AMEN!!

Ready to Go Deeper? (Anti-Racism Activity Guide)

31 Ways You Can Process and Build Upon Your Experience With This Book:

Self-Identification

1. *If you identify as African American*, what's your favorite scenario? Why?
2. *If you identify as bi-racial or multiracial*, which scenarios call your experiences with racism to mind?
3. *If you identify as white*, where did you see yourself in this book?
4. *Picture yourself* in a scenario as the character whom you most resemble from a race, class, gender and age perspective. What might you have done or said differently than that character in that situation?

Stories About Racism

5. *Journal* about which scenarios spoke to you most and why.
6. *Write about the childhood memories* and/or other aspects of your life story that a particular scenario invokes for you.
7. *Choose joy*. If you are African-American, re-examine a scenario that stays with you. Draw, write, or perform the African American character's(s') transformation of a racist moment into a moment of joy. Reflect on how this scenario relates to your own struggle to transform your rage and/or sadness into joy.
8. *Draw* what you think happened before a scenario. Then draw what comes next.
9. *Choose a child character*. Find a different scenario that could represent the next stage in that child's life, and the next stage, and so on. What story does your sequence

tell?

0. *Group the scenarios by the emotions they portray.* What patterns do you see? What emotions portrayed do you relate to most, in which scenarios?
1. *Close your eyes.* Randomly flip through the book. Keeping your eyes closed, open to any illustration on the right side of the book. Wherever your finger lands, write from the perspective of the living being or inanimate object in that scene.
2. *Choose a scenario* that brings to mind a familiar moment in United States history. Tell that story. Explain the connections.

ialogue

3. *Write a letter* to a character in one of the scenarios. What do you think that person needs to hear in that moment? Write the letter the character might write back to you.
4. *Choose a memorable character.* Find a quiet place and study the illustration—its details of body language, expression, objects, and space. Close your eyes. What do you hear the character saying?
5. *Mix and match characters* from different scenarios. For example, tell the story of what a character from one scenario might do and/or say if s/he/they were in a different scenario.
6. *[Partner or group activity]* Choose a scenario with 2 or more characters, assign roles. Use the written dialogue as a script. Read your part. Then extend the scene by improvising your character's actions and words. If your character has no dialogue from the start, improvise all the way through.

Cross-Racial Relationships

17. *If you have a cross-racial relationship* in your life, i.e., family, partner, friend, colleague, etc. What scenarios resonated most with you? Why?
18. *Read and discuss the book in a racial affinity group* as a bridge to share the complexities of your own stories about race and racism. Then invite another racial affinity group of a different racial identification to join you for a cross-racial dialogue about the book.

Workplace Issues of Racism & Race

19. *Suggest the reading of the book in your workplace* as a means of identifying these and/or other scenarios that impact your ability to be an effective team.
20. *Which workplace scenario most strongly resembles your workplace?* What organizational support or culture shift would need to occur to transform that scenario?

White Accomplices

21. *Choose any scenario involving white characters.* What would it look like for one of those white characters or a white character you invent to act as an accomplice in interrupting racism in that scenario?
22. *What conversations can you imagine* white characters from other scenarios having with each other? How can these conversations lead to action that helps to interrupt racism?
23. *Choose a scenario depicting a microaggression* enacted by a white character. If you are a person of the global majority, pretend you are the character absorbing this microaggression. What circumstances might cause you to take the risk of giving the white person in this scenario feedback about their racism? If you are white, think

of a time when you received such feedback about your racism. What clues on the part of the person of the global majority do you have that indicate that your response to their feedback helped to build your relationship?

Community

4. *Discuss the significance of the scenarios with circles of your family, friends, and community.* (This can be either a fun, impromptu event or something more structured and formal, depending on the outcome you are looking for.)
5. *Group the scenarios by age.* What patterns are apparent in each age group?
6. What could *an older African American* character tell or ask *a younger African American* character and vice versa?
7. *Start a study group* in your community about racism, using the book as a conversation launcher.
8. *Choose any scenario.* How could the community where the African American character lives interrupt the oppressions expressed in the illustration? How could a community outside of that character's neighborhood interrupt the oppressions? What community strategies have you been personally involved in? Which have been most successful?
9. Choose a scenario that involves *a character's direct or indirect interaction with an institution* familiar to you. What institutional action steps would need to happen to interrupt the racism the character is experiencing?
10. *Suggest this book as a reading circle book* choice at your place of worship, public library, or institution.
11. *Create a community plan of action.* Use one or more of the scenarios that relate to issues of racism in your community to launch a community discussion regarding a plan of action for anti-racism work.

About the Creators of This Book

About the Author, Anika Nailah

Cultural liberationist, fiction author, performance poet, an former instructor at Wheaton, Cambridge, and Smith co leges, Anika Nailah is the founder/former director of Books Hope, a Boston-area program that helps young people writ publish, and sell their own books. Residing in New Englan she provides social justice consulting, authoring services, an writing coaching. This is her first time writing a book with a illustrator, and she is so glad she did!

Feel free to contact her at anikanailah.com. She would love t hear from you.

About the Illustrator, C. Andrew Williams

Originally from South Carolina, Carlton Andrew Williams has always had a passion for drawing and telling stories. He's been inspired by many things--animated movies and tv shows, comics, and video games--which, as an adult, he still enjoys(in the time he has left between his work, art, and social life).

He also co-authors and co-illustrates an online comic called *Tripod*, on Instagram. He received a BA in Media Arts from The University of South Carolina in 2009, and an MFA in Illustration from the Academy of Art University in 2016. He currently lives in Oakland, California.

You can find his personal sketches and drawings on Instagram, @cawdraw!

CPSIA information can be obtained
at www.ICGtesting.com
Printed in the USA
BVHW09s1540170918
527656BV00012B/41/P